30 Days of Praise and Thanksgiving

BRENDA K. RICE

Fulton Books
Meadville, PA

Published by Fulton Books 2022

ISBN 978-1-63985-784-5 (paperback)
ISBN 978-1-63985-785-2 (digital)

Printed in the United States of America

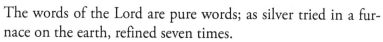

The words of the Lord are pure words; as silver tried in a furnace on the earth, refined seven times.

—Psalms 12:6 (NIV)

To my grandmother, who was an incredible prayer warrior and an example of what it looks like to have a true relationship with God. Also, my husband who always has my back. Of course, my children, their mates, and my grandchildren; what a joy they are in my life. But most of all, to God who led me to write this book, to Him be all the glory.

Taken from NIV scriptures.

God never changes. His word is pure and does not change. How comforting is that I can rely on that everyday of my life. God is immutable never changing always the same.

This is my story of COVID virus and what happened. My husband and I were confined to our vacation home in the mountains of North Carolina, because of the COVID virus spreading in the US. The mask came on, and the constant washing of hands started. And not being able to go anywhere except to grocery, pick food up, or have it delivered. Life was changing at a pace that was hard to understand. It was as though God stopped time.

So during this time, God and I had plenty of time to be together without interruptions. I really felt a leading to write down scriptures that praised God. I started in the Psalms. David, a man after God's on heart, knew how to praise God. The Psalms are full of praises. When it comes down to it, how can we praise God in a way He deserves? And what I came to understand is His word is pure. My mind could never think up these beautiful words of praise to my Father. A God who is creator and sovereign Lord.

When I think about who I am, I'm just a dot on the face of this earth. God deserves so much more than the words that come out of my mouth. I'm just a sinner saved by grace. But He chose me, and He knew me before the foundation of the earth. I'm just in awe of that. He drew me to Him, and I was saved. Only because of what Jesus, His son, did in dying for me. That is the only way to the Father God. It's a free gift. In John 3:16–17, it says,

For God so loved the world that He gave His only begotten Son that whoever believes in Him shall not perish but have eternal life. For God did not send His Son into the world to condemn the world, but to save the world through Him.

I found that the true praising of God is the pure food of His word, the Bible. In using these passages of praise in my quiet time, it opened up my heart to Him and my faith, to fellowship with Him.

For you, who are just a new believer or more seasoned believer, maybe you find yourself in starting your time with God a little confusing at times. I find praying God's word back to Him is a beautiful way to know Him. For He delights in the praises of His people.

How can we praise a God that is so far above our thinking? That's the question. In the quiet of this COVID isolation, the Holy Spirit led me to write this book. This is for you to read and pray back to God, to encourage you and lift your spirits. It will make you more thankful in praising him each day.

Sometimes, I wondered how can God use me, a sinful person, to write this. I think about the apostle Paul and how God changed him and used him for His kingdom work. I'm so grateful God changed me and is still changing me. I've found when you're totally surrendered to Him, then you know that you can be used for His work.

Sometime, I go into my time with the Lord in the morning, half awake. But I know if I just start reading these praise verses and praying them back to Him, the Holy Spirit will awaken me to my God. There are times when I just don't feel like it, or my mind is wandering, so I just keep at it. Then, I have a breakthrough. "Satan, our enemy, is a master at causing confusion and he hates it when you praise God." When Satan is trying to distract me, I determine to keep my mind focused on praising God. As Gods word says, God inhabitants the praises of his people. Psalm 22:3 Oswald Chambers said in his book, *The Utmost for His Highest*, that it is impossible to exhaust God's love, and it is impossible to exhaust my love if it flows from the spirit of God within me.

I love this story about the apostle Peter. Jesus asked him, "Do you love Me?" He asked him three times. Did Peter really know how to love God? He has seen Jesus and walked with Him, heard His teaching, and saw the miracles. So the question to me is, how do I love God?

It's just not saying the words. But having that deep love for Him. I've never seen God, touched or hugged Him like the apostles did. How is that possible? The Holy Spirit is my teacher. He teaches me how to love God, through His Written Word, the Bible. It is inspired by Him through man. The Bible is about God, not us. We need to see God in all things, for He is all things—creator, love, mercy, and judge. There are no human words to even touch His greatness, goodness, and beauty. Our finite minds cannot even reach that high. That's why we have the Holy Spirt living inside of us, to give us glimpses of Him.

God wants to have a relationship with us. We need to celebrate God in our everyday life no matter what. The good times and the hard. He is always there, just waiting for us to spend time with Him.

What do we do when life throws us something that's really hard to deal in? We praise, for it gives us hope and faith and trust. So we are to praise in worry, doubt, hurt, and tears. When your heart has been ripped apart in any way, you praise. I heard a story about a man who lost his son, and in the hospital floor, he fell down on his knees and praised God for his son's life. That is praise and knowing who his God is. Life isn't anything unless we seek God. He is the essence of life, my center, and the air I breath. His radiance and beauty are revealed in all things.

Someone asked me how did I learn to study the Bible. I said by opening it up and reading and allowing the Holy Spirit to teach me.

Another tool I use is to write down things I am thankful for and keep a journal of it. For instance,

1. I praise God for life.
2. For Jesus dying for me.
3. Family, home, food, clothing, health, church, the Bible, protection, and friends.
4. My spiritual gifts.
5. A sound mind, wisdom, knowledge, and discernment.
6. For His peace.
7. For His love, mercy, and grace.
8. That He can use me for His kingdom work.

And I can go on and on. Start your list and keep adding to it. God's plan for our life is a good plan, Jeremiah 29:11–13 says,

> For I know the plans I have for you,' declares the Lord, 'plans to prosper you and not to harm you, plans to give you hope and a future. Then you will call upon me and come and pray to me, and I will listen to you. You will seek me and find me when you seek me with all your heart.

Philippians 1:9–10 says,

> And this is my prayer, that your love may abound more and more in knowledge and depth of insight, so that you may be able to decern what is best and may be pure and blameless until the day of Christ.

Colossians 1:9–12 says,

> For this reason, since the day we heard about you, we have not stopped praying

for you and asking God to fill you with the knowledge of His will through all spiritual wisdom and understanding and we pray this in order that you may live a life worthy of the Lord and may please Him in every way: bearing fruit in every good work, growing in the knowledge of God, being strengthened with all power according to His glorious might so that you may have great endurance and patience, and joyfully giving thanks to the Father, who has qualified you to share in the inheritance of the saints in the kingdom of light.

God's word is filled with life. All we are responsible to do is read it and obey it and love it. And our life will be filled with joy.

Praise Day 1

I will give thanks to the Lord according to his righteousness and will sing praise to the name of the Lord Most High. (Psalm 7:17)

O Lord, our Lord, How, majestic is your name in all the earth, who have displayed your splendor above the heavens. (Psalm 8:1)

But you O Lord, are a shield about me my glory, and the One who lifts my head. (Psalm 3:3)

You have put gladness in my heart. (Psalm 4:7)

For it is You who blesses the righteous man, O Lord. You surround him with favor as with a shield. (Psalm 5:12)

My shield is with God who saves the upright in heart. (Psalm 7:10)

I will give thanks to the Lord with all my heart; I will tell of all your wonders. I will be glad and exult in You. I will sing praise to Your name, O Most High. (Psalm 9:1–2)

But the Lord abides forever; He has established His throne for judgement. (Psalm 9:7)

The Lord also will be a stronghold for the oppressed, a stronghold in times of trouble. (Psalm 9:9)

And those who know Your name will put their trust in You, for You, O Lord have not forsaken those who seek You. (Psalm 9:10)

Prayer: Lord, I come into Your presences with thanksgiving and praise. For You are my God who is worthy to be praised in all Your glory and majesty. Teach me how to praise You more all through my day.

Praise Day 2

For the Lord is righteous, he loves righteousness, the upright will behold His face. (Psalm 11:7)

The Lord is in His Holy Temple, the Lord's throne is in heaven. His eyes behold, His eyelids test the sons of men. (Psalm 11:4)

The words of the Lord are pure words: As silver tried in a furnace on the earth refined seven times. (Psalm 12:6)

But I have trusted in your loving kindness; my heart shall rejoice in your salvation. I will sing to the Lord, because He has dealt bountifully with me. (Psalm 13:5–6)

You will make known to me the path of life. In Your presence is fullness of joy; in Your right hand there are pleasures forever. (Psalm 16:11)

I love You, O Lord my strength. The Lord is my rock and my fortress and my deliverer. My God, my rock in whom I take refuge. My shield and the horn of my salvation, my stronghold. I call upon the Lord, who is worthy to be praised, and I am saved from my enemies. (Psalm 18:1–3)

The Lord lives and blessed be my rock; and exalted be the God of my salvation. (Psalm 18:46)

Therefore, I will give thanks to you among the nations O Lord, and I will sing praises to Your name. (Psalm 18:49)

The heavens are telling of the glory of God; and their expanse is declaring the work of His hands. (Psalm 19:1)

Be exalted, O Lord, in our strength; we will sing and praise your power. (Psalm 21:13)

Prayer: Lord, thank You for Your pure word, that tells me about how wonderful You are. And how much You love me. I will praise with all of my heart and lean not on my own understanding. Keep me ever focused on Your plan for my life.

Praise Day 3

For the kingdom is the Lord's, and he rules over the nations. (Psalm 22:28)

The earth is the Lord's and all it contains, the world, and those who dwell in it. (Psalm 24:1)

Who is the King of Glory? The Lord strong and mighty, the mighty, in battle. Who is this King of Glory? The Lord of hosts. He is King of Glory. (Psalm 24:8)

The Lord is my light and my salvation, whom shall, I fear? The Lord is the defense of my life. Whom shall I dread? (Psalm 27:1)

One thing I have asked from the Lord, that I shall seek: That I may dwell in the house of the Lord all the days of my life. To behold the beauty of the Lord and to meditate in His Temple. (Psalm 27:4)

I will sing, yes will sing praises to the Lord. (Psalm 27:6)

I would have despaired unless I had believed that I would see the goodness of the Lord, in the land of the living. (Psalm 27:13)

The Lord is my strength and my shield; my heart trusts in Him, and I am helped; Therefore, my heart exults, and with my song I shall thank Him. The Lord is their strength and he is a saving defense to His anointed. (Psalm 28:7–8)

Ascribe to the Lord, O sons of the mighty. Ascribe to the Lord glory and strength. Ascribe to the Lord the glory due to His name. Worship the Lord in holy array. The voice of the Lord is upon the waters, the God of glory thunders. The voice of the Lord is powerful. The voice of the Lord is majestic. The Lord sits as king forever. The Lord will give strength to His people. The Lord will bless His people with peace. (Psalm 29:1–5, 10–11)

Sing praise to the Lord, you His godly ones, and give thanks to His holy name. (Psalm 30:4)

Prayer: When I think of how powerful You are Lord of all creations, sometimes, it's hard for me to understand. But when I see Your love that poured out in Your Son, Jesus, to us, how awesome that is. Lord, help me to never lose sight of You and Your greatness, love, and peace.

Praise Day 4

You have turned for me my morning into dancing; You have loosed my sackcloth and girded me with gladness, that my soul may sing praise to you, and not be silent. O Lord my God. I will give thanks to you forever. (Psalms 30:11–12)

Sing for joy in the Lord, O you righteous ones; Praise is becoming to the upright. Give thanks to the Lord with thy lips. Sing praise to Him with a harp of strings. Sing to Him a new song. Play skillfully with a shout of joy. For the word of the Lord is upright and all His work is done in faithfulness. By the word of the Lord the heavens were made, and by the breath of His mouth all their host.

Let all the earth fear the Lord; let all the inhabitants of the world stand in awe of Him. For He spoke and it was done; He commanded and it stood fast. The counsel of the Lord stands forever the plans of His heart from generation to generation. The Lord looks from heaven He sees all the sons of men. From His dwelling place He looks out on all the inhabitants of the earth. He who fashions the hearts of them all He who understands all their works. Behold the eye of the Lord is on those who fear Him on those who hope for His loving kindness. (Psalms 33:1–4, 6, 8–9, 11, 13–15, 18)

I will bless the Lord at all times; His praise shall continually be in my mouth. O magnify the Lord with me, and let us exalt His name together. O taste and see that the Lord is good. How blessed is the man who takes refuge in Him. (Psalms 34:1, 3, 8)

Your loving kindness, O Lord, extends to the heavens. Your faithfulness reaches to the skies. Your righteousness is like the mountains of God; Your judgements are like a great deep. O Lord, you preserve man and beast. How precious is Your loving kindness, O God! And the children of men take refuge in the shadows of your wings. For with You is the fountain of life. In your light we see light. (Psalms 36:5–7, 9)

Prayer: Sometimes, I try to visualize You sitting on Your throne in all Your glory and splendor. Looking down on us your creation. What do You see in sinful man? You see Jesus and what He did for mankind. Forgiveness. Lord, I pray You find me faithful to what You have called me to do.

Praise Day 5

He put a new song in my mouth, a song of praise to our God. Many will see and fear and will trust in the Lord. Many, O Lord my God, are the wonders which You have done, and Your thoughts toward us. There is none to compare with You, if I would declare and speak of them, they would be too numerous to count. (Psalms 40:3, 5)

In God we have boasted all day long, and we will give thanks to your name forever. (Psalms 44:8)

Come behold the works of the Lord, who has wrought desolations in the earth. He makes wars to cease to the end of the earth. Cease striving and know that I am God; I will be exalted among the nations I will be exalted in the earth. The Lord of hosts is with us; The God of Jacob is our stronghold. (Psalms 46:8–11)

Shout to God with the voice of joy. For the Lord Most High is to be feared as a great King over all the earth. God has ascended with a shout, the Lord with the sound of a trumpet. Sing Praises to God sing praises, sing praises to our King of all the earth. God reigns over the nations God sits on His holy throne. For the shields of the earth belong to God. He is highly exalted. (Psalms 47:1–2, 5–6, 8–9)

Great is the Lord, and greatly to be praised, in the city of our God, His holy mountain. (Psalms 48:1)

Willingly I will sacrifice to You, I will give thanks to Your name, O Lord, for it is good. For He has delivered me from all trouble. (Psalms 54:6–7)

Be exalted above the heavens, O God; let your glory be above all the earth. (Psalms 57:11)

Prayer: You, my Lord, have delivered me from trouble many times in my life. I thank You that You had a plan for my life before I was born. Forgive me when I was selfish; for I know that it did not please You. But thank You, that You never left me and waited for my return for what You wanted to show me. All I needed to do was obey.

Praise Day 6

When I am afraid, I will put my trust in You. In God whose word I praise. In God I have put my trust; I shall not be afraid. In God whose word I praise. In the Lord, whose word I praise. In God I have put my trust, I shall not be afraid What can man do to me? For You have delivered my soul from death, indeed my feet from stumbling so that I may walk before God in the light of the living. (Psalm 56:3–4, 10–11, 13)

He has sent redemption to His people. He has ordained His covenant forever. Holy and awesome is His name. (Psalm 111:9)

Be exalted above the heavens O God; Let your glory be above all the earth. My heart is steadfast, O God, my heart is steadfast; I will sing, yes, I will sing praises; I will give thanks to You, O Lord among the peoples; I will sing praises to You among the nations. For your lovingkindness is great to the heavens, and Your truth to the clouds. Be exalted above the heavens, O God. Let Your glory be above all the earth. (Psalm 57:5, 7, 9–11)

But as for me, I shall sing of your strength; Yes, I shall joyfully sing of Your lovingkindness in the morning; For you have been my stronghold, and a refuge in the day of my distress. O my strength, I will sing praises to You. For God is my stronghold, the God who shows me lovingkindness. (Psalm 59:16–17)

My soul waits in silence for God only. For my hope is from Him. He only is my rock and my salvation my stronghold, I shall not be shaken O God my salvation and my glory rest. The rock of my strength my refuge is in God. That power belongs to God. And lovingkindness is Yours, O Lord. For You recompense a man according to his work. (Psalms 62:5–6, 11–12)

To see Your power and Your glory. Because Your lovingkindness is better than life. My lips shall praise You. So, I will bless you as long as I live; I will lift up my hands in Your name. My soul is satisfied as with marrow and fatness. And my mouth offers praise with joyful lips. (Psalm 63:2–5)

Prayer: My trust is in You, my Savior. For You are my shield and protector. Show me those areas in my life that I have not surrendered to You and trusted You for. For that is my heart's desire.

Praise Day 7

By awesome deeds You answer us in righteousness, O God of our salvation. You who are the trust of all the ends of the earth and of the farthest sea; who establishes the mountains by His strength, being girded with might; who stilled the roaring of the seas, the roaring of their waves, and the turmoil of the nation. They who dwell in the ends of the earth stand in awe of your signs. You make the dawn and the sunset shout for joy.

You visit the earth and cause it to overflow; you greatly enrich it; the stream of God is full of water; You prepare their grain; for this You prepare the earth. You water its furrow abundantly, you settle its ridges You soften it with showers, you bless its growth. You have crowned the year with Your bounty, and Your paths drip with fatness. The pastures of the wilderness drip, and the hills gird themselves with rejoicing. The meadows are clothed with flocks, and the valleys are covered with grain; they shout for joy, yes, they sing. (Psalm 65:5–13)

Shout joyfully to God, all the earth; Sing the glory of His name. Make His praise glorious. Say to God, 'How awesome are Your works! Because of the greatness of Your power your enemies will give feigned obedience to You. All the earth will worship You, and will sing praises to You. They will sing praises to Your name. Come and see the works of God, who is awesome in His deeds toward the sons of men.

He turned the sea into dry land, they passed through the river on foot there, let us rejoice in Him. He rules by His might forever; His eyes keep watch on the nations let not the rebellious exalt themselves. Bless our God, O peoples and sound His praise abroad. Who keeps us in life and does not allow our feet to slip. For you have tried us O God; You have refined us as silver is refined. Blessed be God, who has not turned away my prayer. Nor His loving kindness from me. (Psalms 66:1–10, 20)

Prayer: You are an awesome God, Creator of all. You make creations so beautiful, so we can enjoy the works of Your hands. Thank You that I have eyes to see that beauty. Help me, Lord, to never lose that joy of seeing a sunrise or a sunset.

Praise Day 8

All kings will bow down to Him and all nations will serve Him. (Psalm 72:11)

All the ends of the earth will remember and turn to the Lord, and all the families of the nations will bow down before me. (Psalm 22:27)

I will bow down toward Your holy temple and will give thanks to your name, for your loving kindness and your truth. (Psalm 138:2)

God be gracious to us and bless us, and cause his face to shine upon us. That your way may be known on the earth. Your salvation among all nations. Let the peoples praise You. Let the nations be glad and sing for joy. For you will judge the peoples with uprightness and guide the nations on the earth. Let the peoples praise you O God, let all the peoples praise You. The earth has yielded its produce. God, our God blesses us. God blesses us, that all the ends of the earth may fear Him. (Psalm 67:1–7)

Sing to God, sing praises to His name; Lift up a song for Him who rides through the deserts. Whose name is the Lord, and exult before Him. Blessed be the Lord, who daily bears our burden, the God who is our salvation. Sing to

God, O kingdoms of the earth sing praises to the Lord.

To Him who rides upon the highest heavens, which are from ancient times; Behold, He speaks forth with His voice, a mighty voice. Ascribe strength to God; His majesty is over Israel and His strength is in the skies. O God, you are awesome from Your sanctuary. The God of Israel Himself given strength and power to the people. Blessed be God. (Psalm 68:4, 19, 32–35)

For you are my rock and my fortress. For You are my hope, O Lord God You are my confidence from my youth. I will also praise You with a harp even Your truth, O my God; to You I will sing praises with the lyre, O holy one of Israel. My lips will shout for joy, and my soul, which You have redeemed. My tongue also will utter your righteousness all day long. (Psalm 71:3, 5, 22–24)

Prayer: Every knee will bow, and every tongue will confess Jesus is Lord. With my mouth, I will praise You and worship You. I know that through Your word, You are teaching me how to love You more and to serve You, in my journey here on earth, until I see You face-to-face.

Praise Day 9

May His name endure forever; may His name increase as long as the sun shines; and let men bless themselves by Him. Let all nations call Him blessed; bless be the Lord God, the God of Israel, who alone works wonder. And blessed be His glorious name forever. And may the whole earth be filled with His glory. Amen and Amen. (Psalm 72:17–19)

Who have I in heaven but You? And besides you, I desire nothing on earth. My flesh and my heart may fail. But God is the strength of my heart and my portion forever. But as for me. the nearness of God is my good. I have made the Lord my refuge, That I may tell of all Your works. (Psalm 73:25–26, 28)

We give thanks to You, O God, we give thanks for Your name is near. Men declare Your wondrous works. But God is the judge; He puts down one and exalts another. (Psalm 75:1, 7)

Sing for joy to God our strength; Shout joyfully to the God of Jacob. (Psalm 81:1)

God takes His stand in His own congregation. He judges in the midst of the rulers. Arise

O God, judge the earth! For it is you who possess all the nation. (Psalm 82:1, 9)

That they may know that you alone whose name is the Lord, are the Most High over all the earth. (Psalm 83:18)

How lovely are Your dwelling places, O Lord of hosts. My soul longed and even yearned for the courts of the Lord. My heart and my flesh sing for joy to the living God. The bird also has found a house and the swallow a nest for herself, where she may lay her young. Even Your altars, O Lord of hosts, my King and my God.

How blessed are those who dwell in your house! They are ever praising you. How blessed is the man whose strength is in you. In whose heart are the highways to Zion. For a day in your courts is better than a thousand outside. For the Lord God is a sun and shield; The Lord gives grace and glory no good thing does He withhold from those who walk uprightly. (Psalm 84:1–5, 10–11)

Prayer: What do I have on earth if I don't have You, Lord? You are my center, my lifeline. Keep me ever close to You, so I will not wander after what the world has to offer.

Praise Day 10

I will give thanks to You, O lord my God, with all my heart, and will glorify Your name forever. For Your loving kindness toward me is great and You have delivered my soul from the depth of sheol. But You, O Lord, are a God merciful and gracious. Slow to anger and abundant in lovingkindness and truth. (Psalm 86:12–13, 15)

Truth springs from the earth, and righteousness looks down from heaven. Indeed, the lord will give what is good, and our land will yield it's, produce. Righteousness will go before Him and will make His footsteps into a way. (Psalm 85:11–13)

The heavens will praise Your wonders, O Lord; Your faithfulness also in the assembly of the holy ones. For who in the skies is comparable to the Lord? Who among the sons of the mighty is like the Lord. A God greatly feared in the council of the holy ones, and awesome above all those who are around Him? O Lord God of hosts, who is like You, O mighty Lord? Your faithfulness also surrounds you. You rule the swelling of the sea; when its waves rise, you still them. The heavens are yours the earth also is Yours; the world and all it contains, You, have founded them.

The north and south, You, have created them. You have a strong arm; Your hand is mighty. Your, right hand is exalted. Righteousness and justice are the foundation of Your throne. Loving kindness and truth go before You. For you are the glory of our strength and by your favor our horn is exalted. For our shield belongs to the Lord, and our king to the Holy One of Israel. My covenant I will not violate, nor, will I alter the utterance of my lips. Once I have sworn by my holiness. I will not lie to David. (Psalm 89:5–9, 11–14, 17–18, 34–35)

Prayer: I love God, that You are immutable. And Your word is sure and does not change. Forgive me when I haven't trusted You in things that I should. Continue to change those things in me that needs an attitude adjustment.

Praise Day 11

Lord, You, have been our dwelling place in all generations. Before the mountains were born or You gave birth to the earth and the world. Even from everlasting to everlasting, You, are God. For a thousand years in Your sight are like yesterday when it passes by, or as a watch in the night. (Psalm 90:1–2, 4)

He who dwells in the shelter of the, Most High will abide in the shadow of the almighty. I will say to the Lord, my, refuge and my fortress, my God, in whom I trust! For it is He who delivers you from the snare of the trapper and from the deadly pestilence. He will cover you with His pinions, and under His wings you may seek refuge; His faithfulness is a shield and bulwark.

You will not be afraid of the terror by night, or of the arrow that flies by day; of the pestilence that stalks in darkness, or of the destruction that lays waste at noon. A thousand may fall at your side and ten thousand at your right hand but, it shall not approach you. You will only look on with your eyes and see the recompense of the wicked. For you have made the Lord my refuge, even the Most High your dwelling place. No evil will befall you nor will any plague come near your tent. For he will give His angels charge concerning you, to guard you in all your ways.

They will bear you up in their hands, that you do not strike your foot against a stone. You will tread upon the lion and cobra the young lion and the serpent you will trample down. Because he has loved me therefore, I will deliver him; I will set him securely on high, because he has known my name. He will call upon me, and I will answer Him; I will be with him in trouble; I will rescue him and honor him. With a long life I will satisfy him, and let him see my salvation. (Psalm 91:1–16)

Prayer: Thank You, God, for Your protection. You are my refuge and fortress. When life gets hard, keep me ever mindful of Your great love for me. And that no weapon formed against me will prosper.

Praise Day 12

It is good to give thanks to the Lord, And, to sing praises to your name, O Most High; to declare Your loving kindness in the morning, and your faithfulness by night. For you, O Lord, have made me glad by what You have done, I will sing for joy at the works of your hands. How great are Your works, O Lord!

Your thoughts are very deep. But You, O Lord are on high forever. The righteous man will flourish like the palm tree He will grow like a cedar in Lebanon. Planted in the house of the Lord, they will flourish in the courts of our God. They will still yield fruit in old age they shall be full of sap and very green. To declare that the Lord is upright He is my rock and there is no unrighteousness in Him. (Psalm 92:1–2, 4–5, 8, 12–15)

The Lord reigns, He is clothed with majesty. The Lord has clothed and girded himself with strength. Indeed, the world is firmly established, it will not be moved. Your throne is established from of old. You are from everlasting. More than the sounds of many waters, than the mighty breakers of the sea the Lord on high is mighty. Your testimonies are fully confirmed. Holiness befits Your house O Lord forevermore. (Psalm 93:1–2, 4–5)

But the Lord has been my stronghold, and my God the rock of my refuge. (Psalm 94:22)

O come let us sing for joy to the Lord, let us shout joyfully to the rock of our salvation. Let us come before His presence with thanksgiving, let us shout joyfully to Him with Psalm. For the Lord is a great God and a great King above all gods. In whose hand are the depths of the earth, the peaks of the mountains are his also.

The sea is His for it was He who made it, and His hands formed the dry land. Come let us worship and bow down, let, us kneel before the Lord our Maker. For He is our God, and we are the people of His pasture and the sheep of His hand. (Psalm 95:1–7)

Prayer: Lord, to worship You, my Creator, is so awesome. To behold Your glory in your splendor, I want to worship the way You deserve from the innermost part of my being. Teach me, Holy Spirit, that kind of worship.

Praise Day 13

Sing to the Lord a new song; sing to the Lord, all the earth. Sing to the Lord, bless His name; proclaim good tidings of His salvation from day to day. Tell of His glory among the nations, His wonderful deeds among all the peoples. For great is the Lord and greatly to be praised.

He is to be feared above all gods. For all the gods of the peoples are idols, but the Lord made the heavens. Splendor and majesty are before Him strength and beauty are in His sanctuary. Ascribe to the Lord, O families of the peoples, ascribe to the Lord glory and strength. Ascribe to the Lord the glory of His name, bring an offering and come into His courts. Worship the Lord in holy attire.

Tremble before Him, all the earth. Say among the nations, the Lord reigns, indeed, the world is firmly established, it will not be moved. He will judge the peoples with equity. Let the heavens be glad and let the earth rejoice. Let the sea roar, and all it contains. Let the field exult and all that is in it. Then all the trees of the forest will sing for joy. Before the Lord, for He is coming. For He is coming to judge the earth. He will judge the world in righteousness. And the peoples in His faithfulness. (Psalm 96:1–13)

O sing to the Lord a new song, For He has done wonderful things. His right hand and His holy arm have gained the victory for Him. The Lord has made known His salvation He as revealed in the sight of the nation. He has remembered His lovingkindness and His faithfulness to the house of Israel; All the ends of the earth have seen the salvation of our God.

Shout joyfully to the Lord, all the earth. Break forth and sing for joy and sing praises. Sing praises to the Lord with the lyre, with the lyre and the sound of melody. With trumpets and the sound of the horn. Shout joyfully before the Lord. Let the sea roar and all it contains. The world and those who dwell in it. Let the rivers clap their hands, Let the mountains sing together for joy. Before the Lord, for He is coming to judge the earth; He will judge the world with righteousness. And the peoples with equity. (Psalm 98:1–9)

Prayer: Lord, You're coming is soon. And I look forward to that day. When You come in all Your glory to take us home, I pray I never lose sight of that. For until then, I will sing praises to You and proclaim Your great name.

Praise Day 14

The Lord reigns let the people tremble. He is enthroned above the cherubim, let the earth shake. The Lord is great in Zion, and He is exalted above all the peoples. Let them praise Your great and awesome name; Holy is He. The strength of the King loves justice; You have established equity; you have executed justice and righteousness in Jacob. Exalt the Lord our God and worship at His footstool; Holy is He. Exalt the Lord our God and worship at His holy hill, for holy is the Lord our God. (Psalm 99:1–5, 9)

Shout joyfully to the Lord, all the earth. Serve the Lord with gladness; come before Him with joyful singing. Know that the Lord is God It is He who has made us and not we our ourselves we are His people and the sheep of His pasture. Enter His gates with praise. Give thanks to Him bless His name. For the Lord is good; His faithfulness to all generations. (Psalm 100:1–5)

I will sing of lovingkindness and justice. To you, O Lord, I will sing praises. (Psalm 101:1)

Bless the Lord, O my soul, and all that is within me, bless His Holy name. Bless the Lord, O my soul, and forget none of His benefits; who pardons all your iniquities, who heals all your diseases. Who redeems your life from the pit. Who crowns you with lovingkindness and compassion? Who satisfies your years with good things, so that your youth is renewed like the eagle.

The Lord is compassionate and gracious. Slow to anger and abounding in loving kindness. For as high as the heavens are above the earth, so great is His lovingkindness toward those who fear Him. As far as the east is from the west so far, has He removed our transgression from us. As a father has compassion on his children, so the Lord has compassion on those who fear him; for He Himself knows our frame; He is mindful that we are but dust.

For the loving kindness of the Lord is from everlasting to everlasting on those who fear Him and His righteousness to children's children. The Lord has established His throne in the heavens and His sovereignty rules over all. (Psalm 103:1–5, 8, 11–14, 17, 19)

Prayer: Thank You, God, that You allow us, Your children, to come into Your courtroom to fall at Your feet and worship You. And Jesus, thank You that You sit at the right hand of God the Father, interceding on my behalf.

Praise Day 15

Bless the Lord, O my soul, O lord, my God, You, are very great. You are clothed with splendor and majesty. Covering Yourself with light as with a cloak, stretching out heaven like a tent curtain. He lays the beams of His upper chambers in the waters; He makes the clouds His chariot. He walks upon the wing of the wind. He makes the winds His messengers flaming fire His ministers. He established the earth upon its foundations, so that it will not totter forever and ever.

You covered it with the deep as with a garment, the waters were standing above the mountains. At Your rebuke they fled, at the sound of Your thunder they hurried away. The mountains rose; the valleys sank down to the place which You established for them. You set a boundary that they may not pass over. So that they will not return to cover the earth. He sends forth springs in the valleys; they flow between the mountains. They give drink to every beast of the field; The wild donkeys quench their thirst. Beside them the birds of the heavens dwell; They lift up their voices among the branches.

He waters the mountains from his upper chambers, the earth is satisfied with the fruit of His works. He causes the grass to grow for the cattle, and vegetation for the labor of man, so that he may bring forth food from the earth. The trees of the Lord drink their fill, the cedars of Lebanon which He planted. He made the moon for the seasons; The sun the place of its settings. You appointed darkness and it becomes night. In which all the beasts of forest prowl about. The young lions roar after their prey and seek their food from God.

O Lord, how many are Your works. In wisdom You have made them all, the earth is full of Your possessions. You send forth Your Spirit they are created; and You renew the face of the ground. Let the glory of the Lord endure forever; Let the Lord be glad in His works; He looks at the earth, and it trembles; He touches the mountains and they smoke. I will sing to the Lord as long as I live; I will sing praise to my God while I have my being. (Psalm 104:1–14, 16, 19–21, 24, 30–33)

Prayer:

Let my meditation be pleasing to Him; As for me, I shall be glad in the Lord. (Psalm 104: 34)

Praise Day 16

Oh, give thanks to the Lord call upon His name. Make known His deeds among the peoples. Sing to Him; sing praises to Him, speak of all His wonders. Glory in His holy name, let the heart of those who seek be glad. Remember His wonders which He has done, His marvels and the judgements uttered by His mouth. He is the Lord our God; His judgements are in all the earth. He has remembered His covenant forever, The, word which He commanded to a thousand generations. (Psalm 105:1–3, 5, 7–8)

Praise the Lord! Oh, give thanks to the Lord, for He is good; For His lovingkindness is everlasting. Blessed be the Lord, the Lord, the God of Israel from everlasting even to everlasting and let all the people say Amen. Praise the Lord! (Psalm 106:1, 48)

Oh, give thanks to the Lord for He is good, for His loving kindness is everlasting. Let them give thanks to the Lord for His lovingkindness, and for His wonders to the sons of men. Let them also offer sacrifices of thanksgiving and tell of His works with joyful singing. (Psalm 107:1, 8, 22)

My heart is steadfast, Oh God; I will sing, I will sing praises even with my soul. Awake, harp and lyre; I will awaken the dawn! I will give thanks to You, O lord among the peoples, and I will sing praises to you among the nations. For Your loving kindness is great above the heavens. And Your truth reaches to the skies. Be exalted, O God, above the heavens, and Your glory above all the earth. (Psalm 108:1–5)

Praise the Lord! I will give thanks to the Lord with all my heart, in the company of the upright and in the assembly. Great are the works of the Lord: They are studied by all who delight in them. Splendid and majestic is His work, and His righteousness endures forever. He has made His wonders to be remembered the Lord is gracious and compassionate.

He has given food to those who fear Him; He will remember His covenant forever. He has made known to His people the power of His works, in giving them the heritage of the nations. The works of His hands are truth and justice all His precepts are sure. They are upheld forever and ever; They are performed in truth and uprightness. (Psalm 111:1–8)

Prayer: Your faithfulness is new every morning. Thank you, Lord.

Praise Day 17

Give thanks to the Lord, for He is good; for His loving kindness is everlasting. It is better to take refuge in the Lord, than trust in man. The Lord is my strength and song and He has become my salvation. The sound of joyful shouting and salvation is in the tents of the righteous. The right hand of the Lord does valiantly.

The stone which the builders rejected has become the chief corner stone. This is the Lord's doing; It is marvelous in our eyes. This is the day which the Lord has made. Let us rejoice and be glad in it. You are my God, and I give thanks to You. You are my God and I extol thee. Give thanks to the Lord, for He is good. For His loving kindness is everlasting. (Psalm 118:1, 8, 14–15, 22–24, 18–29)

At midnight I shall rise to give thanks to You. Because of Your righteous ordinances. (Psalm 119:62)

Give thanks to the Lord, for He is good. For His loving kindness is everlasting. Give thanks to the God of gods, for His loving kindness is everlasting. Give thanks to the Lord of Lords. To Him who alone does great wonders.

To Him who made the heavens. To Him who spread out the earth above the waters. To Him who made the great lights. The sun to rule by day. The moon and stars to rule by night. To Him who smote the Egyptians in their firstborn. And brought Israel out from their midst. With a strong hand and an out-stretched arm. (Psalm 136:1–12)

To Him who divided the Red Sea asun-der, and made Israel pass through the midst of it. But He overthrew Pharaoh and his army in the red sea. To Him who led His people through the wilderness. To Him who smote great kings. And slew mighty kings. Sehon king of the Amorites. Og king of Bashan.

And gave their land as a heritage. Even a heritage to Israel His servant. He remem-bered us in our low estate. And has rescued us from our adversaries. Who gives food to all flesh. Give thanks to the God of heaven. (Psalm 136:13–26)

I will give You thanks with all my heart I will sing praises to You before the gods. I will bow down toward Your holy temple. And give thanks to Your name for Your lovingkindness and Your truth. For You have magnified Your word according to all Your name.

All the kings of the earth will give thanks to You O Lord, when they have heard the words of Your mouth. And they will sing of the ways of the Lord, for great is the glory of the Lord. For though the Lord is exalted, yet He regards the lowly, but the haughty He knows from afar. (Psalm 138:1–2, 4–6)

Prayer: I will celebrate You today. For Your loving kindness is better than life.

Praise Day 18

I will extol you, my God, O king, and I will bless Your name forever and ever. Every day I will bless you, and I will praise Your name forever and ever. Great is the Lord, and highly to be praised, and His greatness is unsearchable. One generation shall praise your works to another, and shall declare Your mighty acts. On the glorious splendor of your majesty and on your wonderful works, I will meditate.

Men shall speak of the power of your awesome acts. And I will tell of Your greatness. They shall eagerly utter the memory of your abundant goodness. And will shout joyfully of your righteousness. The Lord is gracious and merciful slow to anger and great in loving kindness. The Lord is good to all, and His mercies are over all His works. All Your works shall give thanks to You, O Lord, and your godly ones shall bless You. They shall speak of the glory of Your kingdom and talk of your power.

To make known to the sons of men, our mighty acts and the glory of the majesty of Your kingdom. Your kingdom is an everlasting kingdom and our dominion endures throughout all generations. The Lord sustains all who fall and raises up all who are bowed down. The eyes of all look to you, and you give them their food in due time. You open your hand and satisfy the desire of every living thing.

The Lord is righteous in all His ways and kind in all His deeds. The Lord is near to all who call upon Him to all who call upon Him in truth. He will fulfill the desire of those who fear Him. He will also hear their cry and will save them. My mouth will speak the praise of the Lord, and all flesh will bless His holy name forever and ever. (Psalm 145:1–19, 21)

He has sent redemption to His people. He has ordained His covenant forever. Holy and awesome is His name. The fear of the Lord is the beginning of wisdom; A good understanding have all those who do His commandments. (Psalm 111:9–10)

Prayer: Lord, You're a holy God to be praised and adored. Thank You that You give us the desires of our heart as we serve You with our gifts. I want to serve You with humility wherever You lead me.

Praise Day 19

Praise the Lord! Praise the Lord O my soul. I will praise the Lord while I live; I will sing praises to my God while I have my being. Do not trust in princes, in mortal man, in whom there is no salvation. How blessed is he whose help is the God of Jacob, whose hope is in the Lord, His God. Who made heaven and earth, the sea and all that is in them; who keeps faith forever. Who executes justice for the oppressed; who gives food to the hungry. The Lord sets the prisoner free.

The Lord opens the eyes of the blind, the Lord raises up those who are bowed down; The Lord loves the righteous; the Lord protects the strangers; He supports the fatherless and the widow, but He thwarts the way of the wicked. The Lord will reign forever, your God, O Zion, to all generation. Praise the Lord! (Psalm 146:1–35, 5–10)

Praise the Lord! O servant of the Lord. Praise the name of the Lord. Blessed be the name of the Lord, from this time forth and forever. From the rising of the sun to its setting the name of the Lord is to be praised.

The Lord is high above all the nations His glory above the heavens. Who is like our Lord our God, who is enthroned on high. Who humbles Himself to behold, the things that are in heaven and in the earth? He raises the poor from the dust and lifts the needy from the ash heap. To make them sit with princes, with the princes of his people. He makes the barren woman abide in the house as a joyful mother of children Praise the Lord! (Psalm 113:1–9)

Not to us, O Lord, not to us, but to your name give glory. Because of Your loving kindness because of Your truth. But our God is in the heavens, He does whatever He pleases O Israel, trust in the Lord, He is their help and their shield.

May you be blessed of the Lord, maker of heaven and earth the heavens are the heavens of the Lord. But the earth He has given to the sons of men. But as for us, we will bless the Lord, from this time forth and forever. Praise the Lord! (Psalm 115: 1, 3, 9, 15–16, 18)

Gracious is the Lord, and righteous: yes, our God is compassionate. In the courts of the Lord's house, in the midst of you, O Jerusalem. Praise the Lord. (Psalm 116:5, 19)

Praise the Lord, all nations: Laud Him all people. For His Loving kindness is great toward us. And the truth of the Lord is everlasting. Praise the Lord! (Psalm 117: 1–2)

Prayer: Lord, my hope is in You, God. You are the source of my being. Lord, help me to help those who are blinded to the truth of who You are. Teach me more about Your love and mercy that's new every morning.

Praise Day 20

Praise the Lord! For it is good to sing praises to our God; for it is pleasant and praise is becoming. The Lord builds up Jerusalem; He gathers the outcasts of Israel. He heals the brokenhearted and binds up their wounds. He counts the number of the stars; He give names to all of them. Great is our Lord and abundant in strength; His understanding is infinite. The Lord supports the afflicted; He brings down the wicked to the ground.

Sing to the Lord with thanksgiving; sing praises to our God on the lyre, Who covers the heavens with clouds, who provides rain for the earth, who makes grass to grow on the mountains. He gives to the beast its food, and to the young ravens which cry. He does not delight in the strength of the horse; He does not take pleasure in the legs of a man. The Lord favors those who fear Him, those who wait for His loving kindness. Praise the Lord, O Jerusalem! Praise your God, O Zion! For He has strengthened the bars of your gates; He has blessed your sons within you.

He makes peace in your borders: He satisfies you with the finest of the wheat. He sends forth His command to the earth; His word runs very swiftly. He gives snow like wool; He scatters the frost like ashes. He casts forth His ice as fragments; who, can stand before His cold? He sends forth His word and melts them; He causes His wind to blow and the waters to flow. He declares His words to Jacob, His statutes and His ordinances to Israel. He has not dealt thus with any nation; and as for His ordinances, they have not known them. Praise the Lord! (Psalm 147:1–20)

Prayer: You heal the brokenhearted and bind up their wounds. That verse has been with me through many things in my life. And it is so true. How You have brought me through so much in my life. And I am so thankful.

Praise Day 21

Praise the Lord! Praise the Lord from the heavens; praise Him in the heights! Praise Him, all His angels; praise Him, all His hosts! Praise Him, sun and moon; praise Him all stars of light. Praise Him, highest heavens, and the waters that are above the heavens! Let them praise the name of the Lord, for He commanded and they were created. He has also established them forever and ever; He has made a decree, which will not pass away.

Praise the Lord from the earth. Sea monsters and all deeps; fire and hail, snow and cloud; stormy wind, fulfilling his word; mountains and all hills; fruit trees and all cedars; beasts and all cattle; creeping things and winged fowl; kings of the earth and all peoples; princes and all judges of the earth, both, young men and virgins; old men and children. Let them praise the name of the Lord, for His name alone is exalted; His glory is above earth and heaven. And He has lifted up a horn for His people praise for all His godly ones; people near to Him. Praise the Lord! (Psalm 148:1–14)

Praise the Lord! Sing to the Lord a new song, and His praise in the congregation of the godly ones. Let Israel be glad in his Maker; let the sons of Zion rejoice in their king. Let them praise His name with dancing; Let them sing praises to Him with timbrel and lyre. For the Lord takes pleasure in His people; He will beautify the afflicted ones with salvation. Let the godly ones exult in glory; let them sing for joy on their beds.

Let the high praises of God be in their mouth, and, a two-edged sword in their hand, to execute vengeance on the nations and punishment on the peoples, to bind their kings with chains. And, their nobles with fetters of iron, to execute on them the judgment written; this is an honor for all His godly ones. Praise the Lord! (Psalm 149:1–9)

Prayer: Let all the heavens and earth praise You, my God, the Maker and giver of all things. For You are, God to be glorified in my life. Thank You that I am Yours.

Praise Day 22

Praise the Lord! Praise God in His sanctuary; praise Him in His mighty expanse. Praise Him for His mighty deeds; praise Him according to His excellent greatness. Praise Him with trumpet sound; praise Him with harp and lyre. Praise Him with timbrel and dancing; praise Him with stringed instruments and pipe. Praise Him with loud cymbals; praise Him with resounding cymbals. Let everything that has breath praise the Lord. Praise the Lord! (Psalm 150:1–6)

'The Lord is my strength and song. And he has become my salvation; this is my God, and I will praise Him; my father's God, and I will extol Him.' 'Who is like you among the gods, O Lord? Who is like you, majestic in holiness, awesome in praise, working wonders?' (Exodus 15:2, 11)

He is your praise and He is your God, who has done these great and awesome things for you, which your eyes have seen. (Deuteronomy 10:21)

'Hear, O kings; give ear, O rulers! I to the Lord, I will sing. I will sing praise to the Lord, the God of Israel.' (Judges 5:3)

How great you are, O Sovereign Lord! There is no one like you and there is no God but you, as we have heard with our own ears. (2 Samuel 7:22)

I call upon the Lord, who is worthy to be praised, and I am saved from my enemies. (2 Samuel 22:4)

Oh give thanks to the Lord. Call upon His name. Sing to him, sing praises to Him speak of all His wonders. For great is the Lord, and greatly to be praised. He also is to be feared above all gods. Ascribe to the Lord the glory due His name; bring an offering and come before Him; worship the Lord in holy array. I give thanks to the Lord, for He is good; for His lovingkindness is everlasting.
They say, 'Save us, O God of our salvation. And gather us and deliver us from the nations. To give, thanks to Your Holy name, and glory in Your praise,' Blessed be the Lord, the God of Israel, from everlasting even to everlasting. Then all the people, said 'Amen,' and praised the Lord. (1 Chronicles 16:8–9, 25, 29, 34–35)

Prayer: When I call upon Your name, You hear my prayer. I praise You for the answer whenever it comes. As great as You are, Your love for me is incredible. Thank You.

Praise Day 23

In unison when the trumpets and the singers were to make themselves heard with one voice to praise and to glorify the Lord, and when they lifted up their voice accompanied by trumpets and cymbals and instruments of music and when they praised the Lord saying, 'He indeed is good for His loving kindness is everlasting,' then the house, the house of the Lord, was filled with a cloud, so that the priests could not stand to minister because of the cloud for the glory of the Lord filled the house of God. (2 Chronicles 5:13–14)

All the sons of Israel, seeing the fire come down and the glory of the Lord upon the house, bowed down on the pavement with their faces to the ground and they worshiped and gave thanks to the Lord, saying, 'Truly He is good, truly His lovingkindness is everlasting. (2 Chronicles 7:3)

With praise and thanksgiving they sang to the Lord. 'He is good, His love to Israel endures forever.' (Ezra 3:11)

He stretches out the north over empty spaces and hangs the earth on nothing. He wraps up the waters in His clouds, and the cloud does not burst under them. He obscures the face of the full moon and spreads His cloud over it. He has inscribed a circle on the surface of the waters at the boundary of light and darkness.

The pillars of heaven tremble and are amazed at His rebuke. He quieted the sea with His power and by His understanding He shattered Rahab. By His breath the heavens are cleared His hand has pierced the fleeing serpent. Behold, these are the fringes of His ways; And, how faint a word we hear of Him! But His mighty thunder, who can understand. (Job 26:7–14)

Counsel is mine and sound wisdom I am understanding, power is mine. (Proverbs 8:14)

The fear of the Lord is the beginning of wisdom. And the knowledge of the Holy One is understanding. For by me your days will be multiplied and years of life will be added to you. (Proverbs 9:10–11)

Prayer: Praise to my Creator of all things. Thank You for allowing me to live in this day. Help me to glorify You in every moment.

Praise Day 24

The name of the Lord is a strong tower the righteous runs into it and is safe. (Proverbs 18:10)

Holy, holy, holy, is the Lord of hosts the whole earth is full of His glory. (Isaiah 6:3)

For a child will be born to us, a son will be given us; and the government will rest on His shoulders; and His name will be called wonderful counselor, mighty God, Eternal Father, Prince of Peace. (Isaiah 9:6)

I even I am the Lord, and apart from me there is no Savior. (Isaiah 43:11)

This is what the Lord says Israel's King and Redeemer the Lord almighty I am the first and I am the last; apart from Me there is no God. (Isaiah 44:6)

I am the Lord, and there is no other. I formed the light and created darkness. I bring prosperity and create disaster, I, the Lord, do this. (Isaiah 45:5–7)

By myself I have sworn, my mouth has uttered in all integrity a word that will not be revoked before Me every knee will bow, by Me every tongue will swear. (Isaiah 45:23)

All mankind will come and bow down before me, says the Lord. (Isaiah 66:23)

O Lord, You are my God; I will exalt You, I will give thanks to your name. For you have worked wonders. Plans formed long ago with perfect faithfulness. He will swallow up death for all time, and the Lord God will wipe tears away from all faces. And He will remove the reproach of His people from all the earth; For the Lord has spoken. (Isaiah 25:1, 8)

The steadfast mind you will keep in perfect peace, because he trusts in You. Trust in the Lord forever for in God the Lord, we have an everlasting Rock. You have increased the nations, O Lord, You have increased the nations, you are glorified, you have extended all the borders of the land. (Isaiah 26:3–4, 15)

Prayer: Everyone will bow down and worship You. Come quickly, Savior, I look forward to that day. I'm still waiting and watching for Your return.

Praise Day 25

I even I am He who comforts you. Who are you that you are afraid of man who dies. And of the son of man who is made like grass. That you have forgotten the Lord your Maker who stretched out the heavens and laid the foundations of the earth.

For I am the Lord your God, who stirs up the sea and its waves roar the Lord of hosts is His name. I have put my words in your mouth and have covered you with the shadow of my hand, to establish the heavens to found the earth and to say to Zion you are My people. (Isaiah 51:12–13, 15–16)

The Lord is exalted for He dwells on high; He has filled Zion with justice and righteousness. And He will be the stability of our times a wealth of salvation, wisdom and knowledge. The fear of the Lord is his treasure. Now I will be exalted, now I will be lifted up. For the Lord is our lawgiver, the Lord is our King, He will save us. (Isaiah 33:5–6, 10, 22)

'As for me, this is My covenant with them,' says the Lord. 'My Spirit which is upon you, and my words which I have put in your mouth shall not depart from your mouth, nor from the mouth of your offspring, nor from the mouth of your offspring offspring' says the Lord from now and forever. (Isaiah 59:21)

In that day you will say: 'Give thanks to the Lord, call on His name; make known among the nations what He has done, proclaim that His name is exalted. Sing to the Lord, for He has done glorious thing; let this be known to all the world. Shout aloud and sing for joy, people of Zion for great is the Holy One of Israel among you.' (Isaiah 12:4–6)

I am the Lord; that is my name! I will not give my glory to another or my praise to idols. Sing to the Lord a new song, His praise from the ends of the earth, you who go down to the sea, and all who live in them. Let them give glory to the Lord and proclaim His praise in the islands. (Isaiah 42:8, 10, 12)

Prayer: Lord, teach me how to praise You with my voice in praying Your scriptures or singing Your praise. Even in my mind, I can worship You in silence. For You, hear me no matter what.

Praise Day 26

And the ransomed of the Lord will return, they will enter Zion with singing, everlasting joy will crown their heads gladness and joy will overtake them and sorrow and sighing will flee away. (Isaiah 35:10)

Shout for joy O heavens, for the Lord has done this shout aloud, O earth beneath, bursts into song you mountains, you forest and all your trees, for the Lord has redeemed Jacob, He displays His glory in Israel. (Isaiah 44:23)

The people I formed for Myself that they may proclaim my praise. (Isaiah 43:21)

Shout for joy, O heavens, rejoice, O earth, burst into song O Mountains! For the Lord comforts his people and will have compassion on His afflicted ones. (Isaiah 49:13)

And the ransomed of the Lord will return. They will enter Zion with singing everlasting joy will crown their heads. Gladness and joy will overtake them, and sorrow and sighing will flee away. (Isaiah 35:10)

For my thoughts are not your thoughts, neither are your ways my way, declares, the Lord.

As the heavens are higher than the earth, so are my ways higher than your ways and my thoughts than your thoughts.

As the rain and the snow come down from heaven and do not return to it without watering the earth and making it bud and flourish, so that it yields seed for the sower and bread to the eater. So is my word that goes out from my mouth. It will not return to me empty but will accomplish what I desire and achieve the purpose for which I sent it. (Isaiah 55:8–11)

There is none like you, O Lord; You are great and great is Your name in might. (Jeremiah 10:6)

Thus says the Lord, who gives the sun for light by day, and the fixed order of the moon and the stars for light by night Who stirs up the sea so that its waves roar; The Lord of host is His name. (Jeremiah 31:35)

Thus says the Lord who made the earth; the Lord who formed it established it the Lord is His name. (Jeremiah 33:2)

Prayer: You created us to praise You. Praising takes down sorrow and hurt. Teach me to come to You first when I hear of a bad report.

Praise Day 27

Heal me, O Lord, and I will be healed. Save me and I will be saved, for you are my praise. (Jeremiah 17:14)

He made the earth by His power; he founded the world by His wisdom and stretched out the heavens by His understanding. When He thunders, the waters in the heavens roar; He makes clouds rise from the ends of the earth. He sends lightning with the rain and brings out the wind from His storehouses. (Jeremiah 51:15–16)

Ah Lord God! Behold you have made the heavens and the earth by your great power and Your out stretched arm! Nothing is too difficult for you. Who shows loving kindness to thousands, but repays the iniquity of fathers into the bosom of their children after them, O great and mighty God.

The Lord of hosts is His name. Great in counsel and mighty in deed whose eyes are open to all the ways of the sons of men, giving to everyone according to his ways and according to the fruit of his deeds. Who has set signs and wonders in the land of Egypt, and even to this day both in Israel and among mankind; and you have made a name for your self, as at this day.

You brought your people Israel out of the land of Egypt with signs and with wonders, and with a strong hand and with an outstretched arm and with great terror. And gave them this land, which you swore to their forefathers to give them, a land flowing with milk and honey. (Jeremiah 32:17–22)

To you, O God of my fathers, I give thanks and praise. For you have given me wisdom and power; even You have made known to me what we requested of You. For you have made known to us the King's matter. (Daniel 2:23)

But at the end of that period, I, Nebuchadnezzar raised my eyes toward heaven and my reason returned to me and I blessed the Most High and praised and honored Him who lives forever; for His dominion is an everlasting dominion.

And His kingdom endures from generation to generation. Now I, Nebuchadnezzar, Praise and exalt and glorify the King of heaven, because everything he does is right all His ways are just and those who walk in pride He is able to humble. (Daniel 4:34, 37)

Prayer: Lord, keep me ever humble, so I can honor You with my life.

Praise Day 28

You will have plenty to eat, until you are full and you will praise the name of the Lord your God, never again will my people be shamed. Then you will know that I am in Israel that I am the Lord your God, and that there is no other, never again will my people be shamed. And afterward, I will pour out my spirit on all people. Your sons and daughter will prophesy, your old men will dream dreams, your young men will see visions. I will show wonders in the heavens and on the earth, blood and fire and bellows of smoke. (Joel 2:26–28, 30)

'Sovereign Lord,' they said 'You made the heavens and the earth and the sea, and everything in them. You spoke by the Holy Spirit through the mouth of your servant, our father David 'Why do the nations rage and people plot in vain?" (Acts 4:24–25)

For God has shut up all in disobedience so that He may show mercy to all. Oh the depth of the riches both of the wisdom and knowledge of God! How unsearchable are His judgments and unfathomable His ways. For who has known the mind of the Lord, or who became His counselor? Or who has first given to Him that it might be paid back to Him again. For from Him and

through Him and to Him are all things. To Him be the glory forever. Amen. (Romans 11:32–36)

It is written, 'as surely as I live; say the Lord, every knee will bow before me and every tongue will confess to God!' (Romans 14:11)

For I say that Christ has become a servant to the circumcision on behalf of the truth of God to confirm the promises given to fathers. So that the gentiles may glorify God for His mercy, as it is written 'Therefore I will praise you among the gentiles; I will sing hymns to your name.' Again, it says, 'Rejoice, O gentiles with his people.' And again 'Praise the Lord all you gentiles and sing praises to Him, all you people.' (Romans 15:8–11)

Prayer: As I meditate upon Your word, give me revelation knowledge. For it's You, Holy Spirit, that opens my heart to my Lord.

Praise Day 29

God is faithful, through whom you were called into fellowship with His Son, Jesus Christ our Lord! (1 Corinthians 1:9)

But of the Son He says, 'Your throne, O God, is forever and ever, and the righteous scepter is the scepter of His kingdom. You have loved righteousness and hated lawlessness; therefore God your God, has anointed you with the oil of gladness above your companions.' And you Lord, in the beginning laid the foundation of the earth, and the heavens are the works of your hands. But you are the same and your years will not come to an end. (Hebrews 1:8–10, 12)

He says, 'I will declare your name to my brothers; in the presence of the congregation I will sing your praise.' (Hebrews 2:12)

Jesus Christ is the same yesterday and today and forever. Through Him then let us continually offer up a sacrifice of praise to God that is the fruit of lips that give thanks to His name. (Hebrews 13:8, 15)

Is anyone among you suffering? Then he must pray. Is anyone cheerful? He is to sing praises. (James 5:13)

But you are a chosen race, a royal priesthood, a holy nation a people of God's own possession, so that you may proclaim the excellence of Him who has called you out of darkness into His marvelous light. (1 Peter 2:9)

In order that in everything God may be glorified through Jesus Christ. To Him belong glory and dominion forever and ever. Amen. (1 Peter 4:11)

Now to Him who is able to keep you from stumbling, and to make you stand in the presence of His glory blameless with great joy. To the only God our Savior through Jesus Christ our Lord, be glory, majesty, dominion, and authority, before all time and now and forever. (Jude 1:24–25)

Prayer: Jesus, thank you for dying for me, so that I can stand in Your presence forgiven for all my sins and that I am chosen, I'm in awe of that. And that You took me out of darkness into Your light.

Praise Day 30

After this I heard what sounded like the roar of a great multitude in heaven shouting 'Hallelujah"! Salvation and glory and power belong to our God, for true and just are his judgment; He has condemned the great prostitute who corrupted the earth by her adulteries. He has avenged on her the blood of his servants.' And again they shouted, 'Hallelujah! smoke from her goes up for ever and ever.' The twenty four elders and the four living creature fell down and worshiped God, who was seated on the throne and they cried 'amen Hallelujah!'

Then a voice came from the throne saying 'Praise our God, all you his servants, you who fear Him, both small and great!' Then I heard what sounded like multitude, like the roar of rushing waters and like loud peals of thunder, shouting 'Hallelujah! For our Lord God almighty reigns. Let us rejoice and be glad and give Him glory! For the wedding of the Lamb has come, and His bride has made herself ready.'

I saw heaven standing open and there before me was a white horse, whose rider is called Faithful and True. With justice he judges and makes war. His eyes are like blazing fire, and on His head are many crowns. He has a name written on Him that no one knows but He Himself. He is dressed in a robe dipped in blood, and His name is the Word of God.

The armies of heaven were following Him, riding on white horses and dressed in fine linen, white and clean.

Out of His mouth comes a sharp sword with which to strike down the nations. He will rule them with an iron scepter. He treads the wine press of the fury of the wrath of God almighty. On His robe and on His thigh he has this name written: King of Kings and Lord of Lords. (Revelation 19:1–7, 11–16)

Prayer: The end of time, when You return, is going to be so wonderful. Thank You, that I will see You in all Your glory and splendor. For You are my Lord, and I am Yours. And nothing can snatch me out of your hand. For my name is written in the book of life, only because of Jesus dying for me. "Hallelujah!" What a Savior.

Showing Thankfulness

Be continuous in your appreciation of the acts of God in your life. It's given God the glory. In everything, give thanks, good or bad. Always being thankful and wait for Him to perfect His plan in our life. When Jesus was on the earth, He always gave thanks to His Father in hopeless situations. As we have prayed, we are to give thanks for the answer. God's supernatural way will come to pass.

CPSIA information can be obtained
at www.ICGtesting.com
Printed in the USA
BVHW051158230223
659070BV00012B/857